Yaltji Ngayuku Papa?

Where's My Dog?

Yaltji Ngayuku Papa? was created by the kids of Tjuntjuntjara Remote Community School: Thalia Brown-Baird, Zara Brown, William Coleman, Keiran Currie, Maylee Davies, TT Hogan, Jason Walker and Katrina Williams, in collaboration with artists Stewart Ennis and Ange Leech.

Photography: Stewart Ennis

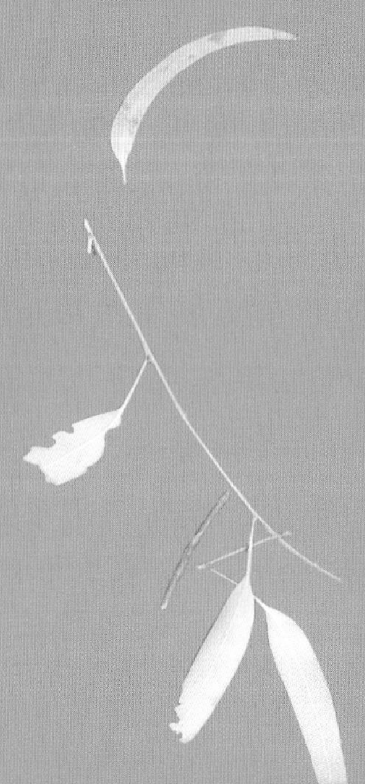

Katju

1

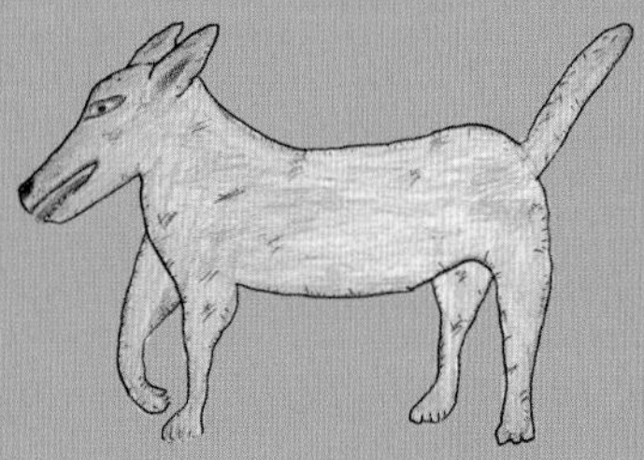

Welcome! This is our school.

Hello! My name is Kililpi. This is my dog, Tjanpi Tjanpi.

Hello!

Kutjara

2

I live in Tjuntjuntjara in Spinifex Country.

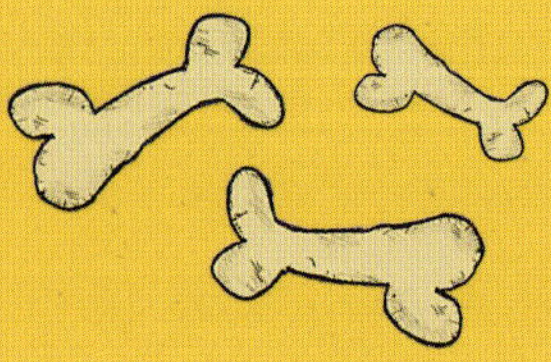

In Pitjantjatjara we count to three. After that we say Tjuta, which means 'many'.

Mankurpa

3

Nyangantja ngayuku malpa.
Palya Kililpi.
These are my friends.
Hi Kililpi.

Tjuta

Nyangantja
Tjuntjuntjarala
papa Tjuta.
Nyangantja
ngayuku papa.
Palya
There are lots
of dogs in
Tjuntjuntjara.
These are
our dogs.

Tjuta
5

Awa Kililpi!
Tjinguru
paluru unngu
Rage Cage.
Yaltji
ngayuku
papa?
Hey Kililpi!
Maybe he's in
the rage cage.
Where's
my dog?

Tjuta

6

Palyru wiya!
He's not here!
Tjinguru paluru unngu oval-pa.
Maybe he's on the oval.
Tjanpi Tjanpi
HART

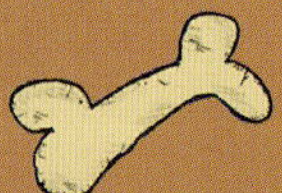

Tjuta

7

Tjinguru paluru unngu the ingka.
Tjanpi Tjanpi
Tjanpi Tjanpi
Palyru wiya.
Palya
Maybe he's in the playground.
He's not here.

Tjuta

8

Where's my dog?

Maybe he's at the store.

Tjuta

9

Where's Tjanpi Tjanpi?

Maybe he's at the Spinifex Arts Centre.

"Punu" is the Pitjantjatjara word for "living wood". This wood comes from Country and is used by the Spinifex people to create wood carvings.

Tjuta

10

Where's
my dog?

Maybe he's
gone bush.

My dog likes
going on
punu trips.

Tjuta

11

Ngayulu
mukuringanyi
palyani punu.
Yaltji ngayuku papa?
Tjinguru Pitjugna
School bus ngka?
Palya
I love
making punu.
Where's my dog?
Maybe he's on
the school bus?

Tjuta

12

He's not here.

Tjanpi Tjanpi!

Tjuta

13

Tjanpi Tjanpi
yaaltji?
Yaltji
ngayuku
papa?
sniff
sniff
sniff
sniff
Have you seen
Tjanpi Tjanpi?
Where's
my dog?

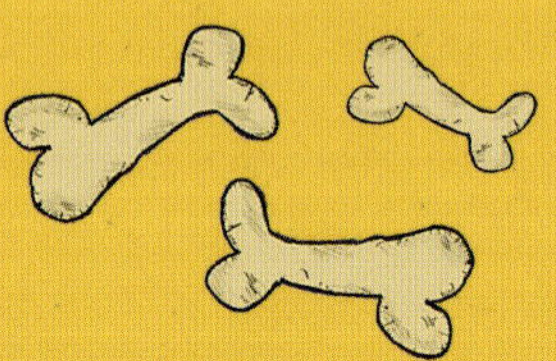

Tjuta

14

Maybe he's at
the dried up river.

Tjuta

15

Tjanpi Tjanpi!
Tjanpi Tjanpi!
Tjanpi Tjanpi!
Tjanpi Tjanpi!
Palyru wiya.
Palya

He's not here.

Tjuta

16

Tjanpi Tjanpi!
Yaaltji?
Ngayulu
paku.
Zzzzz
Tjanpi Tjanpi!
Where are you?
I'm tired.

Tjuta

17

Hey!
There's my dog!

Tjuta

18

Tjanpi Tjanpi! Hurrah!

Tjuta

19

Nyangantja Tjuntjuntjarala papa Tjuta.
Tjuntjuntjarala mungangka kilipi tjuta ngaranyi.
Palya.
There are many dogs in Tjuntjuntjara.
And the Tjuntjuntjara sky has many stars.
Goodnight.

Tjuta

20

The following poem was written
during the Tjuntjuntjara workshop
that led to the creation of this book.

THE DESERT DOGS OF TJUNTJUNTJARA

A Tjuntjuntjara desert dog
is howling at the moon.
Just one at first, then more join in
this ancient howling growling tune.
    [Don't ask me why.
    It's the just their way.
    They've done it every single day
    since dogs began!]
And very, very soon,
the entire yip-yap yelping mob,
the whole red-dirt platoon
of Tjuntjuntjara desert dogs
will be howling at the moon.

The Pitjantjatjara language used in this book is as the Community explained and edited it. Aboriginal languages traditionally have been orally spoken and the text is written as the authors best saw fit.

Mira-Maru

Clowie

LBI

Kungka

Kiana

Twinkles

Angel

Kuti

Tjanpi Tjanpi

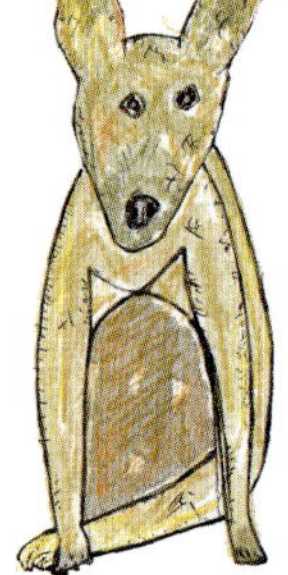

Army boy

Little dog

Blackie

Short tail

Army girl

ACKNOWLEDGEMENTS

Brownie boy

Thanks to:
Tjuntjuntjara Remote Community School Teachers.
Kendrea Hogan and Janine Hogan for Pitjantjatjara–English Translation.
Spinifex artists Maureen Donegan and Gregory Donaldson (for featuring in book).
The Tjuntjuntjara Community Families.
The Pila Nguru Aboriginal Corporation Rangers (for the Punu Bush Trip).

And special thanks to the following Tjuntjuntjara dogs who feature in this book:
Tjanpi Tjanpi aka Kuti, Angel, Army Boy, Army Girl, Blackie, Brownie Boy, Bully, Clowie, Kiana, Kungka, Kuti, LBI, Little Dog, Mima, Mira-Maru, Narshi, One Side, Rocky, Short Tail, Twinkles, Wifi and many more who prefer to remain anonymous.

About the Indigenous Literacy Foundation

The Indigenous Literacy Foundation (ILF) is a national charity working with Aboriginal and Torres Strait Islander remote Communities across Australia. We are Community-led, responding to requests from remote Communities for culturally relevant books, including early learning board books, resources, and programs to support Communities to create and publish their stories in languages of their choice.

First published in 2024 by the Indigenous Literacy Foundation
Gadigal Country
Level 17/207 Kent Street Sydney NSW 2000
ilf.org.au

The project supported by DUAL Australia Pty Ltd.

Cataloguing-in-Publication details are available from the National Library of Australia
www.trove.nla.gov.au

ISBN 9781923179301

Typesetting and design by Stewart Ennis and Justine Taylor
Printed by RR Donnelley Asia Printing Solutions Limited